Finland's Fine Delicacies

Add Culture to Your Cuisine

BY: Ivy Hope

Copyright © 2020 by Ivy Hope

IVY HOPE
COOKBOOK

Copyright/License Page

Please don't reproduce this book. It means you are not allowed to make any type of copy (print or electronic), sell, publish, disseminate or distribute. Only people who have written permission from the author are allowed to do so.

This book is written by the author taking all precautions that the content is true and helpful. However, the reader needs to be careful about his/her action. If anything happens due to the reader's actions the author won't be taken as responsible.

Table of Contents

Introduction 5

1. Karelians Karjalanpiirakka 7

2. Leipäjuusto 10

3. Traditional Savonian Kalakukko 13

4. Korvapuusti 16

5. Heavenly Lihapullat 19

6. Finland's Tasty Sausage Soup 22

7. Mustikkapiirakka 25

8. Salmiakki Candies 28

9. Finnish Salmon Soup 31

10. Lihapiirakka 34

11. Vispipuuro 37

12. Makaronilaatikko 39

13. Split Pea Soup 42

14. Kaalilaatikko 45

15. Piparkakku 48

16. Perunarieska 52

17. Healthy Rosolli 54

18. Nakkikastike With Boiled Potatoes 57

19. Omenalortsy 60

20. Finnish Fruit Jelly 63

21. Pannukakku 65

22. Merimiespata 68

23. Bask on The Finnish Christmas Pastry 71

24. Rye Bread 74

25. Laplands Sautéed Reindeer Delight 77

26. Uudet Perunat Ja Silli 80

27. Sima 83

28. Lakkakakku 86

29. Classic Finnish Easter Mammi 90

30. Munkki 93

Conclusion 96

About the Author 97

Author's Afterthoughts 98

Introduction

Did you know, Finland is known as the happiest country in the world? We believe that one of the greatest contributors to their happiness level is their healthy and scrumptious cuisine. Finnish cuisine is like a paradise for all kinds of eaters. Their luscious dishes are known for impeccably satisfying everyone. Like the scrumptious potato dishes for vegans, the luscious fruit cakes and pies for vegetarians, and not to forget the mind-blowing stews for non-vegetarians. Every delicacy included in this book is to die for. The best part? Since their main ingredients are agro-based products, the food is not only downright succulent but also extremely fresh and nourishing.

If you're unable to decide on which dish suits you best, then you're in luck. This recipe book will give you the perfect tour of the 30 most popular Finnish dishes that are a must-try. Each of these 30 recipes brings in a unique flavor and is so savory that you'll be obsessed. Share the joy with your friends and family by giving them a taste of these yummy dishes. Once they get a taste of these toothsome dishes, they won't be able to stop themselves.

Every recipe mentioned below is extremely simple to prepare and can be whipped up in no time using the most basic food items that are easily available everywhere. So, put on your chef hat and get ready to work some magic. All you need to do is follow the simple steps listed below. Get ready to win some hearts!

1. Karelians Karjalanpiirakka

Karjalanpiirakka is also known as the Karelian's pastry or Karelian's pie since it originated in the region of Karelia. Karjalanpiirakka traditionally consisted of a rye crust with a thick rice porridge filling. It is the most commonly consumed snack in the country. This delicious pastry is very filling and has just a few calories. The stuffing is so delicious that it's hard to believe it's just rice. It can be served for breakfast or even as an evening snack. Rush to your kitchen and get ready to bake some luscious healthy pasties!

Ingredients

- 2 ½ cups of water
- 2 cups of milk
- 1 cup of white rice (uncooked)
- ¼ cup of all-purpose flour
- 1 cup of rye flour
- 1 tsp of salt
- 3 tbsp of butter (melted)
- Salt (to taste)

Serving Size: 16

Preparation Time: 50 mins

Instructions

1. In a saucepan over medium heat, combine the water and rice.

2. Allow 2 cups of water to boil and then lower the heat. Place the lid and simmer it till the water gets absorbed, for about 20 minutes.

3. Now add the milk, lid and simmer for 20 minutes until the milk is absorbed too. Add some salt.

4. Heat the oven to 450° F beforehand.

5. Whip together the rye flour and salt in a medium bowl. Mix in ½ cup of water. Now add in the flour using 1 tbsp at a time while stirring continuously until the dough is no longer sticky. Then separate the dough into 16 even parts.

6. Sprinkle a surface with some flour and roll the dough parts out in the shape of thin circles with a diameter of about 6 inches.

7. Now stuff 3 tbsps. of rice mix in the middle of each of these circular pieces. Even out the mixture leaving out 1 inch from the edges.

8. Fold upward the edges of these pieces and scrunch the edges. To slightly give them the shape of a boat pinch the edges at either end.

9. On an ungreased baking sheet, place these pastries at a distance of about 3 inches. Brush the top of these pastries with some butter.

10. Place them in the preheated oven and bake for about 10-15 minutes till the rice porridge gets a slightly brown color on the top and the crust is firm.

11. Serve while warm.

2. Leipäjuusto

Leipäjuusto is also popularly known as the "Finnish squeaky cheese" as it squeaks against your teeth while munching on it. It is usually made of cow milk and is extremely healthy. Since the cheese is baked, it has a cheese bread-like appearance. Leipäjuusto is very delicious and can be consumed in multiple ways. It can be served as breakfast, evening snacks, or even as a dessert. You can also enhance its taste by topping it with cloudberry jelly. You don't have to be a culinary expert to make this delicious cheese. Just follow these simple steps and you'll be amazed.

Ingredients

- 320 ounces of milk
- 1 tbsp of salt
- 1 tbsp of sugar
- ½ tablet of Hanson's Rennet
- 1 tbsp of cornstarch
- 1 tbsp of cold water

Serving Size: 1

Preparation Time: 2 hours

Instructions

1. Heat up the milk in a double boiler up to a temperature of 185° F-194° F.

2. Crush and dissolve the tablet in 1 tbsp of cold water. Keep it aside.

3. Combine the salt, sugar, and cornstarch in a small bowl. Mix them using some warm milk.

4. Once mixed, add the mixture to the rest of warmed milk.

5. Add the dissolved tablet water to the milk and stir it together.

6. Take the broiler off the heat and place it aside.

7. Let the mix gel. Gelification usually takes up to 35-40 minutes until it's solid.

8. Use a spoon to ensure that the milk has qualified.

9. After this, divide the curd in 1-inch lumps. Allow the lumps to be set and separate from the curds for about 10 minutes.

10. Wrap a wet cloth over a nine-inch cake pan and pour the solid mix on it. Gather the edges and squeeze out the whey. Now, take out the cloth and place the lump firmly on the pan.

11. Place it in the oven and bake for about 15 minutes at a temperature of 400° F.

12. Halfway through flip it till either side gets a goldish brown color.

13. Place it on a rack for about 2 hours and let it cool and dry.

14. Keep it in the refrigerator overnight.

3. Traditional Savonian Kalakukko

Kalakukko is a well-known traditional fish pie from the region of Savonia. It has a thick rye bread crust and is stuffed with fish, pork, and bacon. The crispy crust and the soft fish and meat is sure to trigger your taste buds. The bread and fish duo make the pie delicious, nourishing, and very filling. Once you get a taste of this scrumptious fish pie, you'll cook it again and again. Follow a few simple steps to make this luscious delight.

Ingredients

- 1 ⅔ cups of rye flour
- 1 cup of water
- 1 ⅔ cups of whole-wheat flour
- 28 oz fish fillet
- 1 ½ tsp of butter
- 7 oz of bacon
- 2 ⅔ tbsp of cream
- 1-2 onions.
- 1 egg yolk
- Black pepper (ground) (to taste)
- Salt (to taste)
- ½ cup Lard

Serving Size: 8

Preparation Time: 60 mins

Instructions

1. Add a glass of water, salt and butter into the flour and knead it well.

2. Separate them into 2 halves and set aside in a cool place for about 30 minutes.

3. Cut the onions and fry them with the bacon chopped in the shape of small cubes. Now add in the fish and make a mince. Mix in some pepper, cream, and salt.

4. Now add the fish and pork mince filling into 1 half of the dough. Place the second half as a cover and press it down delicately, ensure that it is covered tight.

5. Cover an oven plate with baking paper. Brush the beaten egg yolk on the fish pie and then place it on the plate.

6. Bake it over a moderate temperature for around 3 hours.

7. After certain long intervals brush it with some lard.

8. You can brush some melted butter on the fish pie pieces while serving.

4. Korvapuusti

Korvapuusti is the Finnish word for cinnamon rolls. They are made of fluffy and sweet cardamom bread and stuffed with cinnamon and sugar that will make your heart skip a beat. Cinnamon rolls taste best with hot tea or coffee which makes them the perfect breakfast or evening- time snack. In addition, the pleasant aroma of cinnamon will already lift your spirits and start your day on a very sweet note. This sweet treat is so delicious that you cannot stop at just one. The cherry on the cake? They are small and can be packed and enjoyed anywhere, anytime. Bless your sweet tooth with this delicious sweet bread by following these few simple steps.

Ingredients

- 1 cup of milk (lukewarm)
- 4-5 cups of all-purpose flour
- ½ cup of sugar
- ¾ cup of brown sugar
- ¼ cup of melted butter
- 2 ¼ tsp of yeast (dry)
- 1 tsp of salt
- 4 tbsp of melted butter
- 1 tbsp of cardamom
- 2 tbsp of cinnamon
- 2 eggs (beaten)
- Sugar for garnish (rock) (to taste)

Serving Size: 14

Preparation Time: 2 hours and 15 minutes

Instructions

1. Mix butter, milk, yeast, and sugar in a large bowl. Let it sit till the yeast starts bubbling for about 10 minutes.

2. Whisk 1 beaten egg, cardamom, and salt and slowly mix in the flour until the dough stops sticking to the sides of the bowl. Knead till the dough is soft, smooth and not very sticky.

3. Place the dough in a greased bowl. Lid it with a cling wrap and set aside to rise for about an hour.

4. Press down the dough and separate it into 2 even halves. Roll either half into a rectangle (8×14). Brush them with the butter and drop in the cinnamon and brown sugar.

5. Begin from the long side and tightly roll either half into a long snake-like structure.

6. Make 7 triangle-shaped rolls from each of the halves by diagonally chopping after every two inches with a knife.

7. Slightly grease a cookie sheet and place these triangular rolls on it with their points upwards and press down on the tips giving them an ear shape. Wrap it with a clean towel and set aside to rise till it's doubled.

8. Heat oven to 400° F beforehand.

9. Now brush each roll with 1 beaten egg and powder with some rock sugar.

10. Bake on the middle rack until it turns to a golden-brown color for about 10-15 minutes.

5. Heavenly Lihapullat

Lihapullat is the Finnish equivalent of the popular meatballs. It is a Finnish favorite, and after you try it, it'll be yours too. After all, who doesn't love meatballs? The delicious ground beef or pork meatballs are like little bits of heaven for meat lovers. Meatballs are rich and filling and can be paired with absolutely anything. The Fins usually pair it with mashed potatoes or lingonberry jam. You don't need to be a sous chef to make these delicious little meatballs. Let us walk you through this simple recipe to prepare these small pieces of delight at home.

Ingredients

- 1 lb. of ground beef
- 1 onion (minced)
- 1 egg
- ¼ cup of breadcrumbs (dry)
- ¼ cup of red wine
- ¼ cup of cream
- 1 tbsp of oil
- 2 tbsps. of flour
- 2 tbsps. of cream
- ½ tsp of nutmeg (grated)
- ½ tsp of salt
- Black pepper (to taste)

Serving Size: 4

Preparation Time: 20 minutes

Instructions

1. Combine ¼ cup of cream and breadcrumbs and set aside for some time.

2. Mix the minced onion, egg, breadcrumbs, and seasoning to the meat.

3. Wet your hands a little and start shaping the mix into small balls.

4. Heat some oil and pan-fry the meatballs until they get a light brown color. Remove the meatballs from the pan once they're done.

5. For the gravy, remove most of the oil and grease the pan with some red wine. Reduce the wine by increasing the heat to the pan.

6. Now drop in the flour and whisk till it's smooth and thick. Add 2 tbsp. of cream and whisk again.

7. Add the meatballs to the gravy pan.

8. The meatballs are now ready to serve.

6. Finland's Tasty Sausage Soup

Siskonmakkarakeitto is Finland's famous fresh pork sausage soup. The sausages are fresh, soft, and absolutely delicious. The spices and vegetables not only make the soup delicious but also super healthy. The soup is thick and luscious, which makes it a great appetizer. Once you get a taste of it, you'll definitely get hooked. It is simple, juicy, and the best way to consume veggies in disguise. The best part? It is super easy to prepare and ready in less than an hour. So, rush to your kitchen and get to it.

Ingredients

- 2 liters of ham/vegetable stock
- 2 bay leaves
- 3 carrots (diced)
- 10 pcs of black peppercorns
- 1 onion
- 4-5 potatoes (diced)
- 1 parsnip (diced)
- ½ head of celery
- ½ swede (diced)
- 1 pound of pork sausage (chopped)
- 1 Small bunch of parsley

Serving Size: 4

Preparation Time: 20 minutes

Cooking time: 30 mins

Instructions

1. Boil the stock, black peppercorns and leaves in a saucepan.

2. Drop in the chopped carrots and swede. After a gap of about 5 minutes, add in the onion, celery, potato, and parsnip.

3. Allow the vegetables to cook well. Once done, drop in the parsley and sausages.

4. Slow the heat to a simmer after adding all the **Ingredients**.

5. Allow the soup to cook until the sausages rise to the top and are cooked well.

7. Mustikkapiirakka

Do you have a sweet tooth? If you do, then you should definitely try the Finnish Mustikkapiirakka. Mustikkapiirakka is famously known as blueberry pie and very famous Finnish dessert. It is mostly made during the summers since it is the season for blueberries. Nothing can be better than blowing off summer steam by munching on this blueberry delicacy! The crispy crust and the fresh and juicy blueberries do make a heavenly combination. Surprise your guests by serving this delicious homemade pie. Let's walk you through the recipe.

Ingredients

- 1 cup of milk
- 3 cups of all-purpose flour
- ⅔ cup of sugar
- ⅓ cup of butter (melted)
- 4 cups of blueberries
- ¼ oz of dry yeast
- 1 large egg
- ½ tsp of salt
- 2 tbsp of almond flour

Serving Size: 1

Preparation Time: 1 hour 15 minutes

Instructions

1. In a mixer bowl, combine the dry yeast with the warm milk.

2. Drop-in half of the flour, egg, sugar, and salt.

3. Whisk on slow speed till it is combined well and has a smooth texture.

4. Now drop in the butter and the flour, a bit at a time leaving small intervals between them for about 5 minutes till the dough is smooth and only a little sticky.

5. Grease a bowl and add the dough in it, put the lid on and allow it to rise for about an hour until it doubles up.

6. Heat the oven to 350° F.

7. Mix the blueberries with the almond flour in a separate bowl.

8. Lightly flour your hands, on a (12×8 inch) baking sheet press the dough to completely fill the pan and pinch a ridge on the upward lining of the dough.

9. Now smear the blueberry mix on the dough.

10. Bake in the middle rack of the oven until the dough turns goldish brown for about 30 minutes.

11. The blueberry pie is now ready to serve.

8. Salmiakki Candies

Are you someone who prefers salted candies over sweet ones? Try out these Salmiakki candies, and you won't be disappointed. Salmiakki is a Finnish salty licorice confectionery item that will trigger your taste buds. Salty licorice is an acquired taste. Not everyone appreciates it initially, but the astringent, salty taste grows on you. Before you know it, you'll be binging on these salty treats. They can be enjoyed alone as well as with cream, alcoholic beverages, or even meat! So, what are we waiting for? Let's get to it.

Ingredients

- ¼ cup of heavy cream
- ¼ cup of brown rice syrup
- ½ cup of sugar (granulated)
- 4 tbsp of butter (unsalted)
- 2 tbsp of molasses
- 1 tbsp anise extract
- 6 tbsp of whole-wheat flour
- ½ tsp of salt
- Flaky sea salt (to taste)

Serving Size: 36 pieces

Preparation Time: 20 minutes

Instructions

1. Line a (9×5×3 inch) pan with parchment paper on the bottom and sides.

2. Cut the parchment paper to make 36 parchment wraps. (3 ½ × 2 inches).

3. Add sifted whole wheat flour in a small bowl and keep it aside.

4. Boil the heavy cream, syrup, sugar, butter, molasses, and salt in a large saucepan whisking constantly with a spatula till the mix reaches the temperature of 255° F for about 20-25 minutes.

5. Once the temperature is reached take it off the heat. Add in the anise extract and flour and whisk thoroughly till the mix is smooth.

6. Now carefully pour the licorice on the parchment.

7. Allow the licorice to cool down and then sprinkle the sea salt on it.

8. Lid and refrigerate.

9. Once the licorice is completely cool, place it on a cutting board along with the parchment.

10. Cut the licorice with a lightly oiled knife into 6 pieces each, longwise (½ inch) and crosswise (1 ½ inch).

11. Now wrap the licorice strips with the parchment paper and seal the ends.

12. Your salty licorice treats are now ready to serve.

9. Finnish Salmon Soup

We've got great news for all the sea-food lovers out there! Lohikeitto, also popularly known as Finnish salmon soup, is a gift for your taste buds. The creamy soup with soft salmon fillets, potatoes, leeks, and dill will blow your mind! This soup is a blessing in disguise for the days when you're too worn out or lazy, as you can whip it together in no time. A surprise guest visit? Put together this luscious soup within half an hour and win their heart. Salmon soup is also the best way to feed your kids something nourishing and delicious at the same time. What are you waiting for? Gather the ingredients, and let's get to it.

Ingredients

- 1 lb. of salmon filet (reserve the skin)
- 1 lb. of russet potatoes (diced)
- 1 large leek (sliced)
- 1 large carrot (sliced)
- 5 cups of fish stock/water
- 1 cup of fresh dill (chopped finely)
- 1 cup of heavy cream
- 4 tbsps. of butter (unsalted)
- ¼ tsp of allspice
- Salt (to taste)
- Pepper (to taste)

Serving Size: 4

Preparation Time: 35 minutes

Instructions

1. In a soup pot, melt the butter and fry the leeks until they're soft for about 10 minutes.

2. Meanwhile, in a separate saucepan boil together water and the previously set aside fish skin, upon boiling lower the heat and bring it to a simmer for about 10 minutes. Strain and add it to the soup pot.

3. Add the carrots, potatoes, and half of the dill to the soup pot. Allow it to cook until the potatoes are soft for about 10 minutes.

4. Now drop in the cream, allspice and salmon lumps into the soup and allow it to cook thoroughly by simmering over low heat, for a couple of minutes.

5. Drop in the remaining dill. Add some salt and pepper for taste.

6. Serve while hot.

10. Lihapiirakka

Are you fond of pies, or do you prefer meat? If it's hard for you to pick just one, then don't! The Fins have blessed the world by combining two of our most favorite things together. They have blessed the world with their scrumptious meat pie, locally known as Lihapiirakka. Lihapiirakka is Finland's local delicacy and the most famous street food, and it is available everywhere. The crunchy doughnut exterior and the tender, tasteful rice and meat stuffing together make a killer combination! You can have Lihapiirakka for breakfast, evening snacks, or even as a late-night bite. Follow this simple recipe, and you will be able to enjoy this mouthwatering pie within the comfort of your home.

Ingredients

For the dough:

- 1 ¼ cup of lukewarm milk
- 1 egg
- ½ cup of sugar
- 4 ½ cups of flour (white)
- 1 tsp of salt
- ½ cup of butter (melted)
- 2 ¼ tsp of dry yeast

For the meat stuffing:

- 2 pounds of ground beef
- ½ cup of onion (chopped finely)
- 1 cup of rice (pre-cooked)
- ½ cup of parsley (chopped finely)
- 1 tsp of salt
- ½ tsp of pepper

Serving Size: 2

Preparation Time: 1 hour 20 minutes

Instructions

1. Cook the rice in a rice cooker.

2. Cook together the onion and beef, drop in the pepper, salt, and parsley for taste.

3. Now combine the cooked rice with the beef mix. Keep it away.

4. For the dough, stir together the lukewarm milk and yeast and allow it to sit until foamy for about 15 minutes.

5. Blend the yeast mix, melted butter, eggs, sugar, and salt. Drop in the flour a bit at a time and start kneading.

6. Let the dough rise for 1 hour in the bowl. Lid it with a warm towel.

7. Once the dough is done, make small circles (4 inches diameter) of the dough with your hands.

8. Stuff the meat mix in the middle of every circle and seal by pressing the sides with your thumbs.

9. Brush each piece with the beaten egg mix.

10. You can let the pie rise for an hour before putting it into the oven. (optional)

11. Heat the oven to the temperature of 400° F.

12. Bake the pie until it gets a golden-brown color for about 20 minutes.

13. Your meat pies are ready to be served.

11. Vispipuuro

The Fins have a huge variety of rich and delicious desserts. One of the most famous among them is the Vispipuuro. Vispipuuro is a sweet semolina porridge made of lingonberries. You can enjoy this sweet delight without feeling guilty at all, as it is made of fresh fruit and is very nourishing. Surprise your kids with the toothsome porridge that is very healthy and super easy to put together. Let's learn to prepare this divine porridge from scratch.

Ingredients

- 1 liter of water
- ⅔ cup of sugar
- 7/8 cup of semolina
- 1 ⅓ cup of lingonberries
- ¼ tsp of salt

Serving Size: 4

Preparation Time: 55 mins

Instructions

1. Boil the water in a saucepan.

2. Smash the lingonberries and drop them into the saucepan along with the salt and sugar. Allow it to boil for about 10 minutes.

3. Strain it and add it back to the saucepan.

4. Now drop in the semolina and whip thoroughly. Lower the heat and let it cook it for 15 minutes.

5. Keep it away and allow it to cool.

6. Once cooled, whisk it with a hand mixer till it becomes light.

7. You can garnish the porridge with some lingonberries.

12. Makaronilaatikko

Makaronilaatikko is a very popular everyday dish in Finland. It is popularly known as the Finnish macaroni casserole and very similar to the American Mac and Cheese. Bask in the enticing combination of baked macaroni, cheese, and beef. After all, no one can resist the charm of macaroni and minced meat. Do you know what makes this dish even more special? It is very cheap and can be prepared within an hour. So, wait no more. Once you make this recipe, you will, without a doubt, become obsessed with it!

Ingredients

- 8 ounces of dried macaroni
- 5 ounces of cheddar cheese (shredded)
- 1 pound of ground beef
- 3 eggs
- 1 medium onion (diced)
- 2 cups of milk
- 1 tbsp of butter (unsalted)
- 1 - 1 ½ tsp of salt
- ½ tsp of ground black pepper
- ¼ tsp of nutmeg (grated)

Serving Size: 6

Preparation Time: 10 minutes

Instructions

1. Heat the oven to 435° F beforehand.

2. Boil some salted water along in a large pot. Drop in the dried macaroni. Cook and whisk after certain intervals till the noodles are semi-firm and not completely tender.

3. Drain the macaroni and keep aside.

4. Meanwhile, in a large pan, melt the butter over medium heat. Drop in the onion and allow it to cook, whipping it after intervals till it's soft. Whip in the ground beef and break up the pieces once they brown. Sprinkle some salt, nutmeg, and pepper. Once cooked thoroughly, set aside.

5. Add the beef mix to the cooked macaroni and put it in a large oven dish.

6. Combine the eggs and milk in a separate large bowl and pour it over the macaroni and beef. Add some shredded cheese evenly on the top of the macaroni.

7. Now bake in the oven for about 30 minutes until it's golden in color and slightly risen.

8. Your macaroni casserole is ready.

13. Split Pea Soup

The split pea soup is also Hernekeitto in Finland. This soup is popularly consumed as a Thursday tradition besides some pork. Apart from the Finnish culture, the split pea soup is famously consumed in a lot of other cultures, too, with minor changes in the recipe. The split pea soup is made of fresh or dried peas and cooked with some pork, onion, and spices. Hernekeitto has a very high nutritional value. Due to the peas and the meat, this soup is also very filling.

This soup is very appreciated by the Finnish elders, serve this soup to your older relatives and friends as they're sure to love it. Let's walk you through the recipe.

Ingredients

- 8 cups of water
- 1-2 tsp of salt
- 1 bay leaf
- 1 onion
- 1 lb. of whole-grain peas (dried)
- 1 lb. of smoked ham (with bone)
- Pepper (to taste)

Serving Size: 6-8

Preparation Time: 15 minutes

Instructions

1. Place the peas in a colander and clean and drain them.

2. Over medium-high heat, simmer the water and peas in a pot.

3. Chop the onion and drop it in the pot.

4. Drop the bone and the ham in the pot.

5. Sprinkle the salt, pepper, and bay leaf.

6. Boil the soup for around 2 hours till the peas begin to split.

7. If you wish, chop some carrots and potatoes and add them to the soup.

8. Once the ham is appropriately cooked it will separate from the bone. Take out the bone and the ham. Chop the ham into small slices and return it to the pot.

9. Keep adding more salt as the peas will absorb the salt while cooking.

14. Kaalilaatikko

Kaalilaatikko is basically a Finnish cabbage casserole mixed with meat. It consists of two layers of cabbage with a layer of meat in the middle. Savor the taste of the extraordinary combination of the crunchy and fresh cabbage with the tender and juicy meat. There's no better way to feed the finicky eaters some veggies in disguise than to surprise them with some Kaalilaatikko. This dish tastes so heavenly that every layer of this delicious casserole will make you moan with pleasure. Get ready to transform the otherwise bland and simple cabbage into something enticing and irresistible with the help of this luscious recipe!

Ingredients

- 1 pound of ground beef
- 2 beaten eggs
- 1 cabbage head (shredded)
- ½ cup of milk
- 1 cup of fresh breadcrumbs
- 2 tbsps. of butter
- 2 tbsps. of brown sugar
- 1 tsp salt
- ¼ tsp marjoram

Serving Size: 12

Preparation Time: 1 hour 5 minutes

Instructions

1. Heat the oven to 375° F beforehand.

2. Butter a baking dish. (9×13 3-qt)

3. Pour water in a large pot and add the cabbage to it.

4. Boil and simmer till the cabbage is soft yet crispy for about 5 minutes.

5. Drain it. Add the marjoram, butter, ½ tsp of the salt, corn syrup and whisk thoroughly.

6. In a separate bowl, combine together the ½ tsp of salt, eggs, milk, breadcrumbs, and beef.

7. In a large pan, lay half of the cabbage mix. Now cover the cabbage layer by patting and placing the moist meat mixture over it. For the third layer, spread the rest of the cabbage over the meat mixture. Your casserole is now assembled.

8. Bake without a cover till the meat is cooked thoroughly for 45 minutes.

15. Piparkakku

Piparkakku is Finland's most popular gingerbread cookies flavored with cinnamon and cardamom. These cookies are extremely flavorsome and are usually enjoyed during the Christmas season. After all, nothing screams Christmas more than the enticing aroma of cinnamon and cardamom filling the house. Savor these cookies with some hot coffee while opening your Christmas presents, all cuddled up next to the Christmas tree. To add to the festive feeling, you can also cut these cookies in the shape of snowflakes, wreaths, bells, and other Christmas decor. These yummy cookies will definitely be the highlight of your Christmas brunch. Let's keep the Finnish tradition going!

Ingredients

- ¼ cup of golden syrup
- 2 cups of all-purpose flour
- ½ cup of sugar (granulated)
- ½ cup of butter (unsalted)
- 1 egg (beaten)
- 2 tsp of ground ginger
- 1 ¼ of cinnamon
- ½ tsp of pepper
- 1 tsp of ground cloves
- 1 tsp of ground cardamom
- ½ tsp of ground nutmeg
- ½ tsp of salt
- 1 tsp of baking soda

Icing:

- 3 egg whites
- ¼ cup of cold water
- 5 cups of sifted icing sugar
- ¼ tsp of white vinegar

Serving Size: 30 pieces

Preparation Time: 30 minutes

Instructions

1. Over medium heat, blend together the salt, spices, sugar, butter, and syrup in a saucepan. Whisk for 2 minutes until the mixture gets a smooth texture and the butter is melted. Set aside and let it cool for 15 minutes.

2. In a separate bowl, combine the flour and baking soda. Add the syrup mixture and egg and whip until well mixed. Separate into half and cover with plastic wrap. Level into flat disks and keep it in the refrigerator for an hour until it's firm.

3. Heat the oven to 325° F beforehand.

4. Coat 2 baking sheets with parchment paper.

5. Sprinkle some flour on a separate large parchment paper. Roll a disk of dough (⅛ inches thick).

6. Carve out shapes with the help of cookie cutters (2 ½ × 4 inches). Reroll the scraps and refrigerate depending on your needs.

7. Place on the lined baking sheet and bake for 12-14 minutes till the edges turn brown in color. Allow it to cool for about 5 minutes then transfer to the rack. Repeat this process with the remaining dough.

8. For the icing, take a large bowl and whip the vinegar and egg whites using an electric blender set on medium till it's foamy. Now add the sugar and whip until well mixed.

9. Now, change the speed to medium-high and whip for 2 minutes until the mixture thickens. Add some water to thin.

10. To decorate the cooled cookies, pour the mix into a piping bag with a small plain tip.

11. Allow it to sit at room temperature for about 4 hours till the icing hardens.

12. Your cookies are now ready to serve.

16. Perunarieska

Perunarieska is commonly known as potato flatbread. Potato is the main ingredient in a number of Finnish dishes, including Perunarieska. Thanks to these soft and delicious potatoes, Perunarieska appears different and tastier than other bread. The crispy dough on the outside and the soft, juicy mashed potato on the inside create a luscious combination. This scrumptious bread is extremely rich and filling. Unlike other bread, Perunarieska can be eaten separately too. You can enjoy this amazing bread for breakfast, tea time snack, or even for dinner. Topping this bread with some butter works great magic. Follow these few simple steps to make this toothsome and flexible snack.

Ingredients

- 10 ounces mashed potatoes
- 1 pinch of salt
- 1 cup of flour
- 1 large egg

Serving Size: 4 pieces

Preparation Time: 25 minutes

Instructions

1. Heat oven to 425° F beforehand.

2. Combine the egg, flour, salt, and mashed potatoes.

3. Now, separate the mixture into 4 even portions.

4. Coat a baking sheet with baking paper, lay the portions on the baking sheet. Lightly flour your fingers and level each portion into a round, flat disk.

5. Use a fork to prick the bread.

6. Now place it in the oven and bake for about 15 minutes.

7. Your Perunarieska is ready to serve. You can also serve it with butter, fresh dill, and smoked salmon.

17. Healthy Rosolli

Christmas in Finland is impossible without this traditional Rosolli. Rosolli is a delicious salad made from chopped and cooked vegetables especially beetroot, potato, carrot, and onions. All the ingredients perfectly complement each other, making this one of the best salads you will ever have. This scrumptious cold salad can be eaten as a side dish or even as a main dish. It is very filling and exceptionally full of nourishment. The luscious whipped cream highly elevates the taste of the salad and makes it irresistible for everyone, including the finicky kids. Gather all the ingredients, and let's get to cooking.

Ingredients

- 4 boiled potatoes
- 1 gherkin (chopped)
- 4 boiled carrots
- 1 small onion (diced)
- 4 boiled beets
- White pepper (to taste)
- Salt (to taste)

For the Dressing:

- ⅔ -1 cup of whipping cream
- 1 ½ tsp of sugar
- 1 ½ tsp of Water in which the beets were cooked
- 1 ½ tsp of apple cider vinegar

Serving Size: 4-6

Preparation Time: 40 minutes

Instructions

1. Cook the vegetables in advance along with the skin until soft and allow them to cool down.

2. Peel the vegetables and dice them into small equal cubes.

3. Chop the gherkin.

4. Combine the gherkin and the vegetables. Sprinkle it with some white pepper and salt.

5. Lightly stir the cream and sprinkle it with some vinegar, sugar and a few drops of the liquid the beet was cooked in for color.

6. Serve the dressing besides the salad.

18. Nakkikastike With Boiled Potatoes

Nakkikastike is a traditional Finnish homemade hotdog sauce. Just imagining the tender sausages floating in the thick brown sauce flavored with tomato paste, carrots, onion, and cream will make you drool. To add to this heavenly taste, you can serve it along with some boiled or mashed potatoes. This tangy sauce is well-loved by people of all ages, be it your grandparents or your grandchildren, everyone will fall in love with it. After all, who doesn't love sausages? Once your guests get a taste of this succulent sauce, they will be circling around you for the recipe. So, let's learn to prepare this mouthwatering sauce from scratch.

Ingredients

- 1 pack of hot dogs or wieners (sliced)
- 2 cups of chicken broth
- ½ onion (chopped)
- 2 garlic cloves (minced)
- 1 carrot (chopped)
- 2 tsp of butter/ghee
- 1 tsp of brown mustard
- 1 pinch of nutmeg
- ½ tsp of salt
- 1 tbsp of tomato paste
- ½ tbsp of black pepper

Serving Size: 4

Preparation Time: 30 minutes

Instructions

1. Over medium-high heat, warm 1 tsp of butter in a skillet.

2. Drop in the hot dog and fry for about 3 minutes until it gets a brownish color. Take off from the heat and keep away.

3. Lower the heat to medium, drop in the remaining 1 tsp of butter, onion, and carrot and fry for about 5 minutes until soft.

4. Now, drop in the garlic and fry for a minute till you get the aroma, add the tomato paste, mustard, chicken broth, pepper, nutmeg, and salt.

5. Lower the heat to medium-low and simmer for about 20 minutes until darkened.

6. Pour into the blender and blend until smooth then pour it back into the skillet.

7. Sprinkle salt and pepper for taste.

8. Now drop in the hot dogs and simmer for 1-2 minutes before serving.

19. Omenalortsy

Omenalortsys are apple doughnuts that originated in Finland. The crunchy doughnut exterior stuffed with soft stewed apples is a blissful combination. The fresh and juicy taste of the apples makes these doughnuts stand out. You can enjoy these treats for dessert, as well as for snacks. Surprise your kids with these savory and sweet treats. Thanks to this recipe, you can revel in these delicious treats within the comfort of your home. Sharing the steps to this crispy delicacy.

Ingredients

- ¾ cup of flour (self-raising)
- ½ cup of milk
- ¼ cup of powdered sugar
- 2 tbsp of icing sugar
- 1 egg (beaten)
- 2 Fuji Apples
- Pinch of Salt
- Ground cinnamon (to taste)

Serving Size: 4

Preparation Time: 15 minutes

Instructions

1. In a medium bowl, strain the sugar, flour, and salt.

2. Blend together the egg, milk and add it to the flour mixture. Now beat till the batter gets a thick, smooth texture.

3. Now, peel and core 2 apples. Trim and slice them in such a way that each apple produces 8 round slices.

4. Dip each apple slice into the batter and shimmy off the extra batter.

5. Deep fry the slices, a few at a time, on either side until it puffs up and gets a goldish color for about a minute.

6. Place the fried apple doughnuts on a wire rack and sprinkle the top with strained icing sugar and cinnamon.

7. Your apple donuts are not ready to serve!

20. Finnish Fruit Jelly

Kiisseli is Finland's most-loved fruit jelly. It is made of the sweet juice of berries and thickened with potato flour. It is a fresh, luscious, and nourishing dessert. Kiisseli is also extremely versatile. You can enjoy this fresh fruit jelly as a drink as well as a dessert, depending on how you choose to make it. It can also be served both hot or cold and still taste exceptional. Along with all these qualities, this fruit jelly can also be served as a topping on ice creams or pancakes. Grab your favorite berry, and let's get to it.

Ingredients

- 1 cup raspberry or any berry of your choice (fresh or frozen)
- 2 ½ cup of water
- ¼ cup of sugar (scant)
- 2 tbsp of potato flour

Serving Size: 4

Preparation Time: 15 minutes

Instructions

1. In a pot over medium heat, heat the berries and the water together. Whisk the berries to transform them into a sauce form.

2. Slowly add the sugar for taste and blend well. The dessert is supposed to be tart and not sweet.

3. Let the mixture cool down a little. Once it's a little cooler drop in the potato flour and blends until the mix is thick. The perfect texture is as thick as a soup and slightly thinner than jelly.

4. Allow it to cool down.

5. You can choose to serve it with cream or coconut cream as per your taste.

21. Pannukakku

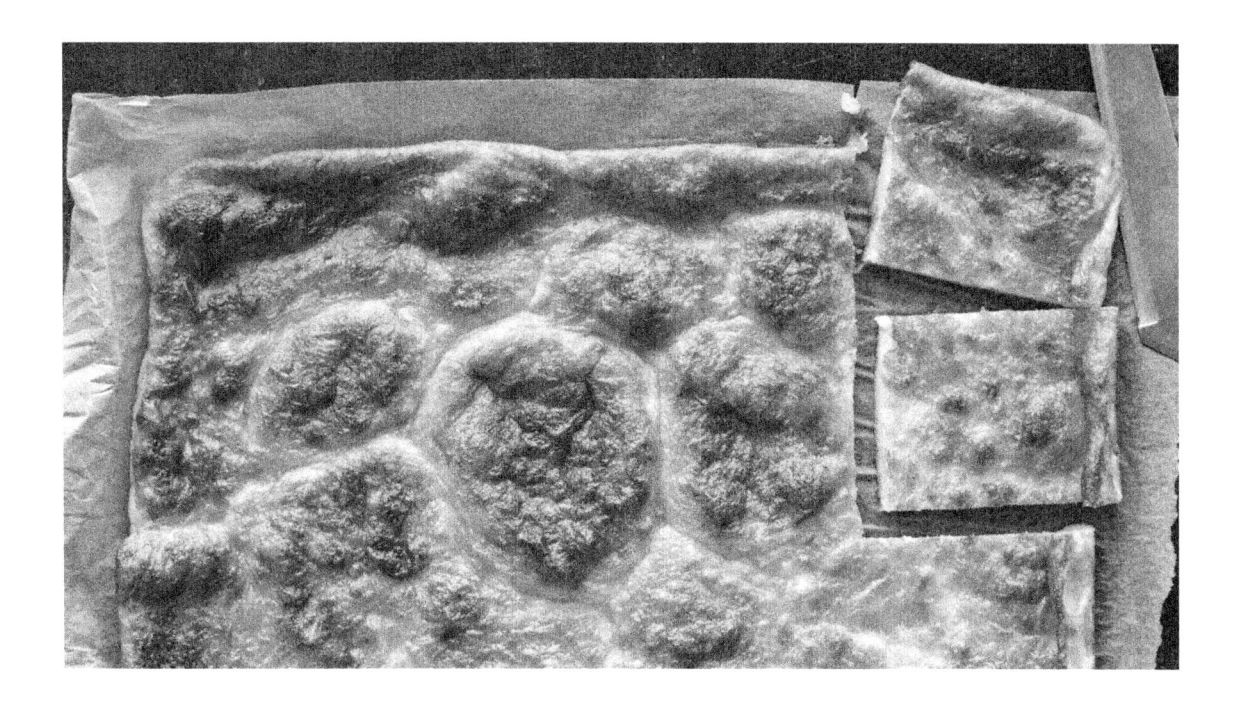

Pannukakku is the Finnish equivalent of pancakes. The only twist the Fins added is that these pancakes are oven-baked. They are traditionally served with berries, whipped cream, or even vanilla ice cream. Apart from being a great dessert, Pannukakku is also an amazing breakfast or evening time snack. Start your day with these delicious and filling pancakes that will already make the day seem happier. Serving it with some hot tea or coffee only adds to its taste. Let's learn to bake these oven-baked pancakes.

Ingredients

- 6 eggs
- 1 ½ cups of all-purpose flour
- 1 ½ cups of milk
- ¼ cup of white sugar (optional)
- ⅓ cup of butter
- 1 tbsp of vanilla extract/sugar
- 1 tsp of baking powder
- ⅛ tsp of lemon zest (grated)
- 1 tsp of salt

Serving Size: 5-6

Preparation Time: 35 minutes

Instructions

1. Combine together the milk, sugar, vanilla sugar, and eggs in a bowl until creamy. Whip in the lemon zest.

2. Strain together the baking powder, salt, and flour in a separate bowl. Pour it into the egg mix and combine. Let the batter sit for around 30 minutes.

3. Heat the oven for 450° F beforehand.

4. Melt some butter in a baking sheet but do not let it brown.

5. Now coat the baking sheet evenly with the melted butter, sides included.

6. Add the pancake batter to the hot, buttered pan and place it in the oven.

7. Bake until it's golden in color and puffed up for about 15 minutes.

22. Merimiespata

Merimiespata is Finland's famous sailor's stew. Just taking a look at the **Ingredients** will make your mouth water. The main ingredient is the delicious and tender sliced beef partnered up with the heavenly potatoes and onions. This already tempting dish is further flavored by spices like allspice and bay leaf. This recipe also uses beer broth to further elevate its taste. After all, beer and beef make a divine combination! Every bite of this delicious stew is so tender and juicy that it melts in your mouth. Charm your guests with this incredible stew! Let's get cooking.

Ingredients

- 3 pounds of boneless roast beef (cut in cubes)
- 8 ounces of fresh mushrooms (packaged)
- 12 fluid ounces of can beer
- 1 cup of all-purpose flour
- 2 cups of beef broth
- 1 tsp of black peppercorns
- 1 tbsp of vegetable oil
- 2 tbsp of soy sauce
- 2 onions (sliced)
- 2 carrots (sliced)
- 1 large potato (sliced)

Serving Size: 8

Preparation Time: 30 minutes

Instructions

1. Heat oven to 350° F beforehand.

2. Keep the beef cubes in a container or a bag full of flour and shake till the meat is evenly coated.

3. Over medium-high heat, pour the oil into the skillet and heat it.

4. Take out the meat from the bag/ container after shimmying off the extra flour. Add the beef cubes to the oil and allow them to fry until they're browned on every side. Drain the oil by placing them on some paper towels.

5. On the lowest rack of a casserole dish (3 quarts), arrange the potatoes and then keep the beef above the potatoes and wrap them with the mushrooms and carrots.

6. Now, pour the beef broth, soy sauce, and beer on the potato and beef dish. Drop the peppercorns on it.

7. Let it bake in the oven without a cover until the meat is soft for about 2 hours.

23. Bask on The Finnish Christmas Pastry

Christmas in Finland is incomplete without these little angelic star-shaped pieces. The tarts are made of crispy, puffy, cheesy dough topped with the toothsome prune jam. If you have a soft spot for sweets, then you can also sprinkle some iced sugar on these little pastries. You will be astonished by how succulent these little treats taste. After all, Christmas is all about binging on some delicious sweets! To give these cookies a festive, fancy, and appealing appearance, they are cut out in the shape of small stars. Let's bask in the festive feeling by enjoying these scrumptious tarts.

Ingredients

For the dough:

- 3 - 3 ½ cups of flour
- ¼ cup of milk
- 1 cup of butter
- 8 ounces of carton cottage/cream cheese
- 1 tsp of salt

Prune stuffing:

- 1 lb. of pitted prunes
- ½ cup of sugar
- 3 cups of water

Serving Size: 24 tarts

Preparation Time: 55 minutes

Instructions

1. Use a pastry blender to combine all the dough ingredients.

2. Pour the milk in the dough to soften it.

3. Separate the dough into 2 large balls or 4 small ones.

4. Wrap the dough and refrigerate overnight.

5. Now for the stuffing, cook the prunes in water until they become tender.

6. Drain the water and puree in a blender.

7. Drop some sugar into the prune puree and mix well.

8. Roll out the dough in the shape of a large square and cut small squares (3 inches) from it. Add a mound of stuffing in the middle of the small squares.

9. Up to ½ inch of the center, split each and every corner.

10. Bend one half of every corner to the middle, it should appear like a pinwheel or a star.

11. Arrange the star tarts on an ungreased baking plate and dust some sugar over it.

12. Keep it aside for about 10 minutes before placing it in the oven.

13. Heat the oven to 400° F and bake the tarts in the hot oven till they're lightly golden brown in color for about 10 minutes.

14. Take out of the oven and allow it to cool on the rack.

24. Rye Bread

Ruisleipä is Finland's most famous yet traditional rye bread. It is one of the very important dishes in Finnish cuisine and is served with almost every meal. It is high in fiber and a great source of nourishment. In contrast to other bread, this bread contains less oil and isn't sweet. It can be enjoyed alone as well as served beside any main dish. The bread is crispy, delicious, and it also complements every dish that it is served beside. Another reason why it is extensively used is that rye bread has a very high storage potential as it doesn't spoil soon. So, what are you waiting for, follow these simple steps to make some luscious rye bread at home!!

Ingredients

- 2 cups of stone ground dark rye flour
- 1 cup of buttermilk
- 1 & ¼ cups of all-purpose flour
- 3 large eggs
- 2 tbsp of baking powder
- 1 tbsp of dark molasses
- 5 tbsp of butter (unsalted)
- 1 tsp of salt
- 1 tsp of whole fennel seeds/ caraway seeds (optional)

Serving Size: 8

Preparation Time: 30 minutes

Instructions

1. Heat the oven to 400° F beforehand.

2. Grease a loaf pan with butter.

3. Whip together the flour and the salt in a bowl.

4. Pour in the buttermilk and add the eggs one by one. Drop in the butter and molasses. Whip slowly until it forms a dough.

5. Drop in the caraway or fennel seeds. (optional)

6. Now, knead the dough for 5 minutes.

7. Place the dough in the greased pan.

8. Place the pan in the oven and bake till it looks like bread and the top has turned brown for about 40 minutes.

9. Allow it to cool on a rack.

25. Laplands Sautéed Reindeer Delight

The popular Sautéed reindeer is known as Poronkaristys in Finland. The delicious sautéed reindeer is the traditional meal of Lapland. It is made of the low fat and strong-flavored meat of a reindeer, seasoned with rich spices. Beer or cream could also be added for taste. This dish is so lush that it will trigger your taste buds. The thin reindeer meat slices are impeccably partnered with some mashed potatoes and lingonberry preserves. The following recipe will help you prepare this savory sautéed reindeer without much effort.

Ingredients

- 2-3 lbs. of reindeer, beef steak
- 1 cup of water
- 2 cloves of garlic
- 1 yellow onion (chopped)
- 2 tbsp of butter
- ½ tsp of ground allspice
- 1 tsp of salt
- ½ tsp of black pepper

Serving Size: 4

Preparation Time: 2 hours

Instructions

1. Keep the reindeer meat in the freezer for 20 minutes before chopping it into thin slices. After slicing, keep it away.

2. Over medium heat, heat the butter in a skillet. Drop in the onion and let it fry for about 6 minutes until tender. Whisk in the garlic, for about 30 seconds, frying until you can smell the aroma.

3. Now, drop in the meat, allspice, salt, water, and pepper and whip thoroughly until well-blended.

4. Allow it to simmer and place the lid over it. Gently simmer by lowering the heat for about an hour until the meat softens.

5. Increase the heat to medium-high and take off the cover. Whip constantly and fry for about 10 minutes until the meat is crisp and dark brown in color and the water gets evaporated.

6. Serve by arranging the meat on top of the layer of mash potatoes along with lingonberry preserves and sliced pickles, sprinkle with some chives.

26. Uudet Perunat Ja Silli

Uudet Perunat Ja Silli is boiled spring potatoes with pickled herrings. The potatoes used in making this delicacy are sweeter and smaller than the usual potatoes and are generally found in abundance during the Finnish summers. This is the reason because of which the dish is exceptionally popular in the summers. This dish can be served as an appetizer or even as a main dish depending on its arrangements and quantity. The juicy and refreshing taste of this dish is also a great way to beat the summer heat. Follow these simple steps to make your summer delight.

Ingredients

- 6 small baby red potatoes
- 3 tbsp of sour cream/ reduced fat
- 2 tbsp of finely chopped red onion
- 1 small container of pickled herring fillets
- Pinch of salt (to taste)
- Pinch of pepper (to taste)
- 1 tbsp of Fresh dill

Serving Size: 2-3

Preparation Time: 5 minutes

Instructions

1. Fill a saucepan with boiling water and steam the potatoes in it till all the potatoes are almost soft and can be penetrated with a fork, for about 15 to 20 mins.

2. Drain and let the potatoes cool down.

3. Chop the potatoes into slices of ¼ inches and sprinkle each slice with a little pepper and salt.

4. Now, chop the herring into ¼ inch slices.

5. Arrange one piece of herring atop each potato slice and add a lump of sour cream on it. Drop some red onion on it and decorate it with the dill.

6. You can also choose to arrange all the ingredients separately beside each other.

7. You can add more pepper if required according to your taste.

27. Sima

Sima is Finland's popular and luscious low alcoholic beverage. This drink is prepared by fermenting a honey or sugar syrup solution. This sparkling drink is flavored using the flesh as well as the rind of lemons. This alcoholic beverage is exceptionally famous and in-demand during the Finnish Vappu festival. Celebrate May Day to the fullest while sipping on this refreshing beverage. Pair this luscious drink with some sweet Munkki, and you'll be blown away with ecstasy. There's no need to purchase Sima anymore. This recipe will allow you to add your own touch and prepare your very own Sima at home.

Ingredients

- 1 gallon of water
- 25 raisins
- 2 large lemons
- ½ cup of sugar (white)
- ½ cup of brown sugar
- ¼ tsp of yeast

Serving Size: 1 gallon

Preparation Time: 20 minutes

Instructions

1. In a large pot, boil the water.

2. Zest 2 large lemons and slice them into small strips, don't forget to remove the seeds.

3. Sprinkle some sugar on the lemons.

4. Once the water is boiled, pour it into a large glass/plastic jar. Drop the sugar and lemon mix in it.

5. Allow it cool until the water is just lukewarm.

6. Now, combine the yeast in it.

7. Place a lid on it and let it keep it away to cool at room temperature till it begins to slightly bubble on the top for about 24 hours.

8. Filter it into a glass jar. Drop in the raisins and sugar. Place it in the refrigerator till the raisins begin to float for about 2-3 days.

9. Serve it while cool.

28. Lakkakakku

Lakkakakku is Finland's celebratory cloudberry cake that originated in Lapland. Today, cloudberry flavored cakes are highly unusual and underrated despite their juicy and savory taste. In this recipe, the luscious cloudberries are soaked in rum, making them even more resistible. This succulent cake consists of four delicious layers of cloudberry preserves and sugary filling, each layer adding a flavor of its own. To make this cake even more enticing and tasty, it is decorated with loads of toothsome whipped cream. The tarty taste of the cloudberries and the sweet sugary taste will make your taste buds explode. The catch? You don't need to be a culinary expert in preparing this cake at home. Follow these simple steps to bring back cloudberry cakes in the market.

Ingredients

- 6 large eggs
- 1 ⅓ cups of all-purpose flour
- 2 cups of cloudberry preserve
- 1 ⅓ cups of sugar (granulated)
- 3 cups of heavy whipped cream
- ½ cup of dark rum
- 3 tsp of pure vanilla extract
- ⅛ tsp of salt
- ¼ cup of confectioner's sugar

Serving Size: 16

Preparation Time: over 1 hour

Instructions

1. Heat the oven at 350° F beforehand.

2. Wrap two 9-inch round cake pans with parchment paper.

3. Break the eggs into a 2-cup measuring jar in order to measure it.

4. Blend the sugar and eggs in a bowl using an electric mixer with a whisk attachment on high speed for about 5 minutes until the mix has a lemon color.

5. Add salt and 2 tsp of vanilla to it. Use a rubber spatula to fold in the flour well rigorously.

6. Pour the batter equally among both the baking pans. Bake for about 25-30 minutes till the cake in the middle region bounces back when touched.

7. Let the pan cool on a wire rack.

8. Once the cake is cooled, slowly remove it from both the pans. With the help of a sharp knife, cut the cake horizontally in such a way that there are 4 layers in total.

9. In order to make the filling, you should whisk the cream until it is firm but not rigid. Now drop in the confectioner's sugar and the remaining 1 tsp of vanilla extract.

10. For arranging the cake: Keep the bottom layer on a plate, brush the rum on top of the cake and smear ⅓ of the filling on it. Place the second layer of the cake on it, brush rum on it and smear ½ of the cloudberry preserves on it.

11. Now, place the third cake layer on it, brush rum on it and smear ⅓ of the filling on it. Finally, place the fourth layer of cake, brush with rum and smear the remaining preserves on it.

12. For decorating the cake, use a pastry bag (12-inch) with a fitted star tip (½- inch) to pipe the rest of the fillings atop the cake in any decorative pattern of your choice.

29. Classic Finnish Easter Mammi

The traditional Finnish Easter is incomplete without a bite of the delicious Mammi. Mammi is Finland's well-known baked rye porridge. The porridge is sweet, scrumptious, and healthy and contains a fair share of proteins. On Easter, Mammi is served with cream, milk, or even with some vanilla sauce, which adds to its taste. Another reason for porridge's popularity is that it doesn't spoil easily and can be refrigerated for days. So, what are you waiting for? Let's celebrate Easter in Finnish style.

Ingredients

- 6 quarts of water
- 1 lb. of malt
- 1-2 tbsp of salt
- 4 tbsp of orange rind (chopped)
- 3 lbs. of rye flour
- ½ cup of Molasses

Serving Size: 2-3

Preparation Time: 1 hour

Instructions

1. Combine together the flour and malt.

2. In a large cooking pan, heat 2 quarts of water with enough of the malt and flour mix in such a way that it forms a thin mixture.

3. Slightly add a layer of flour and malt. Place a lid on the pan and keep it in a warm place for about an hour to sweeten.

4. Combine the sprinkled malt and flour into the mix. Pour more water and then a layer of flour and malt. Allow it to sweeten.

5. Repeat this procedure until you've added the remaining water, malt, and flour.

6. Season by adding the molasses and orange rind along with the last addition of water, malt, and flour. Let it cook for 5 minutes and whisk continuously.

7. Whisk it till it cools.

8. Place it in low oven pans. Don't fill the pan to the brim as the Mammi will rise upon baking.

9. Bake for about 1-2 hours in a moderate oven.

10. Allow it to cool and serve it with milk or cream and sugar.

30. Munkki

Munkki is the Finnish equivalent of doughnuts. These delicious rings are heavily seasoned with cardamom and sugar, making it sweet rings of joy. Doughnuts are a mood changer, one bite of this crispy ring, and you'll become happy already. Munkki is highly associated with the Finnish May Day. No May Day celebration is complete without a drink of Sima and these sugary round doughnuts. Doughnuts are very flexible; they can be served for dessert as well as for teatime snacks. Adding these doughnuts to your menu will surely gain you some extra attention. Nobody can say no to doughnuts! Let's walk you through this simple recipe.

Ingredients

- 1 cup of quark
- 1 quart of canola
- ⅔ cup of water
- ¼ cup of butter (softened)
- ½ cup of sugar
- 4 cups of all-purpose flour
- 1 cube of yeast
- 1 tbsp of cardamom
- 1 tsp of salt
- 1 egg
- ¾ cup of sugar (Garnish)

Serving Size: 16 pieces

Preparation Time: 1 hour 15 mins.

Instructions

1. Mix the water and quart in a small pan and heat at about 100° F until it's lukewarm.

2. In a separate large bowl, blend together the yeast and the quart mix. Whisk them together thoroughly to blend well.

3. Drop-in 2 cups of flour, salt, cardamom, sugar, and egg. Stir thoroughly and then drop 1 ⅓ cup of flour in it along with the butter.

4. Let the dough sit for about 20 minutes.

5. Coat a surface with the remaining ⅔ cup of flour. Place the doughnut batter on this surface and separate the batter into 16 balls.

6. Stretch the balls to make a hole in the center of it, it should appear like a doughnut.

7. Arrange these doughnuts on a cookie sheet and let it sit for about 30 minutes.

8. In the meantime, pour the canola oil, minimum 2 inches deep, in a large shallow pan.

9. Over medium-high heat, heat the oil till its temperature is about 350° F.

10. Now, fry the doughnuts on either side until they are golden brown in color, about 2 minutes per side.

11. With the help of a slotted spoon, take the doughnuts out of the hot oil. Place them on paper towels to drain the excess oil.

12. Allow them to cool slightly and then sprinkle some sugar over them.

13. Serve while warm.

Conclusion

Now that you know exactly how to prepare some rich and extraordinary Finnish dishes, why wait any longer?

Get ready to embark on your own culinary journey with the help of these luscious recipes. Thanks to this recipe book, you now know every popular Finnish dish that you must try! From everyday meals to special occasions, this book covers it all. You needn't wait for an occasion to enjoy these delicacies. All you have to do is, put on your apron, gather these basic ingredients, and follow the simple steps mentioned above. Step aside and watch your loved ones dig into these delicious and exotic dishes. It's your time to shine!

Hyvää ruokahalua!

About the Author

Ivy's mission is to share her recipes with the world. Even though she is not a professional cook she has always had that flair toward cooking. Her hands create magic. She can make even the simplest recipe tastes superb. Everyone who has tried her food has astounding their compliments was what made her think about writing recipes.

She wanted everyone to have a taste of her creations aside from close family and friends. So, deciding to write recipes was her winning decision. She isn't interested in popularity, but how many people have her recipes reached and touched people. Each recipe in her cookbooks is special and has a special meaning in her life. This means that each recipe is created with attention and love. Every ingredient carefully picked, every combination tried and tested.

Her mission started on her birthday about 9 years ago, when her guests couldn't stop prizing the food on the table. The next thing she did was organizing an event where chefs from restaurants were tasting her recipes. This event gave her the courage to start spreading her recipes.

She has written many cookbooks and she is still working on more. There is no end in the art of cooking; all you need is inspiration, love, and dedication.

Author's Afterthoughts

THANK YOU

I am thankful for downloading this book and taking the time to read it. I know that you have learned a lot and you had a great time reading it. Writing books is the best way to share the skills I have with your and the best tips too.

I know that there are many books and choosing my book is amazing. I am thankful that you stopped and took time to decide. You made a great decision and I am sure that you enjoyed it.

I will be even happier if you provide honest feedback about my book. Feedbacks helped by growing and they still do. They help me to choose better content and new ideas. So, maybe your feedback can trigger an idea for my next book.

Thank you again

Sincerely

Ivy Hope

Printed in Great Britain
by Amazon